Stolen Study Companion

Copyright © 2019 by Caroline Klug

Foreword by Robin Prater

All rights reserved. No part of this publication may be reproduced, distributed, or transmitted in any form or by any means, including photocopying, recording, or other electronic or mechanical methods, without the prior written permission of the author, except in the case of brief quotations embodied in critical reviews and certain other noncommercial uses permitted by copyright law. For permission requests, contact the author using the Contact page on www.CarolineKlug.com. Please be sure to include "Permission Request" in the Subject line.

All Scriptures are taken from the Holy Bible, New International Version®, NIV®. Copyright © 1973, 1978, 1984, 2011 from Biblica, Inc.® Used with permission.

Cover design by Tim Fitzpatrick
Author photograph by James Klug

To request Caroline Klug for a speaking event or appearance, please contact the author using the Contact page on www.CarolineKlug.com. Please be sure to include "Event Request" in the Subject line.

ISBN: 978-1-7339008-6-7 (eBook)
ISBN: 978-1-7339008-7-4 (paperback)

Printed in the United States of America

STOLEN
Study Companion

Caroline Klug

A Bible Study Companion

IMPORTANT: Please be sure to read the novel, *Stolen*, in its entirety prior to beginning this study. Knowledge of the end is necessary to fully discuss the components of the allegory it is based on. The novel is sold separately.

Table of Contents

Foreword 8
How to Use This Guide 14
The Allegory 16

Session 1: Walking Among Us 18
Session 2: The Slow Fade 26
Session 3: Under Fire 34
Session 4: Controlling Forces 40
Session 5: Lies We Believe: Fear & Manipulation 48
Session 6: Lies We Believe: Shame & Denial 56
Session 7: Redemption 64

But God 72

Reference Material 76
    Novel Summary 78
    Character Summary 82
    National Helplines 84

FOREWORD

I love reading novels that leave me with something. A nugget, something to ponder, something that causes a change within me. This is just what happened when I read *Stolen*, by Caroline Klug.

Maybe what I love most is that this isn't just a thriller. It isn't just a read for leisure. It's one of those exceptional novels that is woven together with an important message given to us through an allegory. This thriller connects us to these penned words through the verses that come from Colossians 1:13-14: *"For He has rescued us from the dominion of darkness and brought us into the kingdom of the Son He loves, in whom we have redemption, the forgiveness of sins."*

The writing is strong and poignant with a message of hope. When darkness lies all around us, when we feel lost and worthless, He is there to show us His light and make a way for our escape from the darkness into His grace and freedom.

Each chapter travels from past to present that leaves the reader with a constant twist. I have to share that the first few chapters were difficult for me to read. It wasn't the writing.

Caroline Klug

Klug's writing is exceptional. She draws in the reader with such descriptiveness that you can only imagine yourself in the position of the character facing their circumstances and choices. It was the truth in her penned words – the deep and utter brokenness – that moved me. Klug's writing is so descriptive that it brought me to feel the desperation in the characters. Their hearts are open for us to see. Their fear becomes our fear. The terror they feel isn't something made up, but is something very real for thousands each and every day. *Stolen* brings the reader to look outside their own backyard into the world around us that is very real, but can easily be missed if we are not paying attention outside of ourselves.

With Klug's allegory it makes this novel so much more. It brings a message of redemption. We find within these pages characters who believed lies told to them. In fact they believed so much in those lies that they became those lies told. Their choices no longer right and wrong, but what the lie has developed within them. Very much to the degree of just living, taking a breath and trying to survive. This soon is life and they can't imagine anything different.

Something else I love about this novel is that the main character changes her name so no one will know her real name, who she is, or where she came from. The name she goes by is Star. For me, whether or not the author meant this to be huge, it was very poignant for me. Star may have been trying to remain hidden from the world, unknown to everyone around her, but to God, to her Savior, she was a star, one that He knew before, in her present, and would know her future. Whether or not she realized it at the time, she may have not known Him, but He certainly knew Star.

Those lies changed Star. She didn't begin her life as Star but with another name. One that she had forgotten. As the lies became her new life her past faded from memory. She wasn't necessarily trying to forget who she was. She wanted to run away to something better, but one choice led to another and soon her choices were no longer her own. She now became owned by another.

We see characters being held captive. Chains holding them in a darkness. Sex-trafficking is real and it is all around us. It is in our small towns and big cities. Klug brings to light a message that we try to ignore. I applaud her for writing with a purpose. This is one of those novels in which our time invested leaves us with more than we ever expected. At least that's how it was for me. Now more than ever we learn of sex trafficking and the horrors of these girls being kidnapped, now at ages of seven and nine, into a world where nightmares are now reality.

This is one of those novels that will stay with you. At least it has for me. I saw a review that said something along the lines that as a reader she found it hard to understand the characters' choices because she wouldn't have made the same. We tend to think this way when something seems near impossible to us, don't we? We simply can't imagine. Brokenness and lies bring the soul to be held captive into believing we are worthless and useless. We find ourselves in positions we never imagined possible, but there we are and now our next step seems immovable. But then there is love, grace, and mercy. A hand reaching out. Truth seeks us. His hand guides us. There in the midst of our impossible becomes possible through Him.

There's another aspect I loved. A character that isn't seen a great deal within the pages, but his character is so powerful for me: Star's father. This runaway thinks she's forgotten. The lies have told her no one wants her. Her unworthiness has made her an outcast. She's told lies that her father doesn't want her. Never wants to see her again. But what I love is that he never gave up searching. His love remained. A love that was unconditional. He is there with open arms. A father of grace. For me, this was a clear example of our heavenly Father's unconditional love. He's there. Never leaving us.

If we listen to Satan, if we listen to his lies we will soon be believing that we are just as he says. Unloved and unwanted. It is a daily struggle for so many. This is one reason Star never tried to escape her capture. He said he was trying to protect her. Trying to keep her safe away from those who didn't want her and would never believe her. She is no longer running away, but running toward her father. Oh, this picture of grace and redemption stirs my soul. I love that moment she realizes the lies that held her still and remembers the truths within her brings freedom. They may have been buried, covered with deceit, but never absent, always remaining to be brought to light.

We are given a glimpse at this new life. Our main character no longer goes by Star, but her given name. The one that speaks truth of who she really is. As we turn the last page we witness this hope as her new life begins. This is one novel where everything has meaning. A story with a purpose. She is ready and willing to share her story, to touch hearts of others. She is now living with a new outlook. She was saved. Her father waiting with open arms. She wants to live out that same hope to others who are hurting and in need. She wants others to know their worth and that amazing grace she received.

If you're searching for something different, something more than just a good read, I encourage you to grab a copy of *Stolen*. It will take you on a journey to places unexpected and hearts unknown to a place of peace and renewal.

> Robin Prater, Book Reviewer & Blogger
> Taken from her review of the novel,
> *Stolen* by Caroline Klug

Caroline Klug

HOW TO USE THIS GUIDE

IMPORTANT: Please be sure to read the novel, *Stolen*, in its entirety prior to beginning this study. Knowledge of the end is necessary to fully discuss the components of the allegory it is based on. The novel is sold separately.

This seven-session study offers insights into the allegory, and provides discussion questions which can be utilized individually or within a group setting. If using within a group, designate one group member as the leader to facilitate through the content in each session.

Open each session in prayer. This can be done by the group leader, or leader may ask if one of the participants would like to pray.

When done in a group setting, if time is a challenge, participants can choose to read each session introduction and allegory components prior to the group meeting.

SPOILER ALERT: The main character, Galia Gregor, takes on three different names during the course of the book. As we talk about the allegory components, whichever name she went by during the time period we are talking about will be used. For example, when referencing content from Chapter

1, Star will be used. When exploring content from Chapter 20, Galia will be used.

When walking through the allegory, leader should ask the participants if they discovered any other allegory components relative to that session's topic, but not outlined in the study guide. I've outlined the key items, but God may have made something new visible to a reader. If that's the case, I'd love to hear from you on what that is – please use the Contact page on my website: www.CarolineKlug.com.

Make sure to create an environment where individuals feel safe to speak. There are several emotionally heavy topics covered in these sessions, so I'd recommend for the group leader to encourage each participant to share their thoughts, but don't push. Allow individuals the time they need to be comfortable sharing.

Close each session in prayer. You can take this opportunity to ask for prayer requests. Again, this can be done by the leader or any of the participants.

Encourage participants to use the journal space provided to write down any personal thoughts or prayers they may have. This is for personal use, and does not need to be shared with others unless individuals are comfortable doing so.

THE ALLEGORY

For He has rescued us from the dominion of darkness and brought us into the kingdom of the Son He loves, in whom we have redemption, the forgiveness of sins.

Colossians 1:13-14

Caroline Klug

SESSION 1:
Walking Among Us

There are things all around us that influence us for the good, or the not so good. Every day we're required to make choices on what to let in – the music we listen to, the TV programs we watch, the places we go, and the food we eat.

In the same way we care for these things, we also need to be intentional with regard to the people we allow to influence us. We're going to take a look at some of the primary characters from *Stolen*, and understand how their characteristics can be present in our lives through the people around us.

ALLEGORY COMPONENTS

Jack Price
Abductor | Murderer | Liar & Manipulator

> In its simplest form, Jack represents Satan. Satan is a serial killer whose primary goal is to steal, kill, and destroy (John 10:10). Make no mistake – he knows us. He spends time studying us. He knows our weaknesses

and insecurities, and he uses those things to exploit, tempt, and drag us as far from God as he can.

Satan is a master manipulator and, just like Jack did to Star/Sarah, he will try to convince you that the sin of your past or present makes you unworthy, unlovable, and unforgiveable.

Galia Gregor (a.k.a. Star, a.k.a. Sarah)
Friend | Victim | Addict | Slave | Redeemed

Galia represents all of us, at various stages of life. There are points when life seems okay and we get through the day-to-day. Then comes points of attack, and we are rendered helpless. We find ourselves enslaved by the choices we've made and struggling to find a way out. We believe the lies of the enemy and no longer have strength to fight back, accepting defeat as our new normal.

Galia also represents the potential for strength and power when we choose to use our past for God's gain. She shows us the transformation possible when we lift our heads out of the shame of our past sins and use what we've overcome as a beacon to lead others to the light.

Eli Gregor
Father | Forgiver

In many aspects, Eli represents God. It's not a complete representation, as the book character displays some thoughts and feelings which would be contrary to God's character (e.g., feeling responsible for the trauma Galia endured). However, Eli is meant to represent our Heavenly Father who longs to have us in His presence.

When Galia went missing, he searched for her. When she was found, he wept tears of joy. He acknowledged her past choices were not the best ones, but he freely forgave and chose to focus Galia on what was ahead of her, rather than what was behind. This included encouraging her to use her past to help the people in her future.

Teddy Fenton
Friend | Acceptor | Missionary

> Teddy represents light and hope. He's someone who's made it through and understands his place in the greater good. He represents acceptance, not rejection.
>
> Throughout the story, Sarah escapes to thoughts of Teddy – we are wooed by what we know is good, but are often too afraid to walk in that direction. Usually because Satan uses lies to convince us to be afraid or feel unworthy.

Lacey
Roommate | Reporter | Redeemed

> We all know her. She's the friend we bond quickly with over difficult and, usually, shared circumstances. Intentions are typically good, but can be both a positive and negative influence.

There are shared opportunities in every relationship we have. Iron sharpens iron (Proverbs 27:17). We can let them shape us, we can be the positive influence to them, or, as in the case with Lacey and Galia, a mix of both.

Rachel McGinnis
Abductee | Life That Needs Saving

Rachel is an interesting piece of the allegory – one which may not be thought of initially. She represents the harm that can come to others as a result of the consequences of our own actions. Had Galia made the decision to own up to her mistakes and get Jack off the streets five years earlier, Rachel would have never been abducted.

As with all things, God still used it for the good (Romans 8:28). Through those trying circumstances, Rachel was freed from the streets and reunited with her family.

Amy
Runner | Life That Needs Saving

Amy is the girl at the very end of the book, who represents the people around us who are lost and need to hear our stories. They need to be cared for by someone who knows what they are going through, and can see you've made it out of the fire without smelling like it (Daniel 3:27).

Ronny
Criminal | Intimidator | Corruptor

Has there ever been a person in your life who used fear and intimidation to control your choices? This is Ronny. Fueled by his own self-preservation, Ronny is of the mindset of bully or be bullied. He chooses to manhandle and intimidate others before they have the chance to do the same to him.

People like Ronny can rob us of things that are precious to us. They can cause wounds so raw, that they change the entire perception we have of ourselves. These merciless hits to our self-worth cause us to compromise in ways we never imagined we would or could.

TRUTH BEHIND THE LIES

John 10:10
The thief comes only to steal and kill and destroy; I have come that they may have life, and have it to the full.

John 16:33
I have told you these things, so that in Me you may have peace. In this world you will have trouble. But take heart! I have overcome the world.

Proverbs 27:17
As iron sharpens iron, so one person sharpens another.

2 Corinthians 1:3-4
Praise be to the God and Father of our Lord Jesus Christ, the Father of compassion and the God of all comfort, who comforts us in all our troubles, so that we can comfort those in any trouble with the comfort we ourselves receive from God.

REFLECTION QUESTIONS

- What qualities or characteristics do you think make someone a positive influence? Can you think of someone for whom *you* are that positive influence?

- Which one of Galia's stages do you think you're at right now? Friend (moving along day-to-day), victim (experiencing attack), addict (being controlled by something), slave (feeling utterly enslaved by something or someone) or redeemed (walking in freedom)? Why?

- Who in your life might represent our character Amy? What is one thing you could do to reach out to that person and send a message of hope?

- *Privately* think about the key relationships in your life. Are any of those relationships toxic to your personal and spiritual growth? If so, pray and ask God for guidance on how to handle those relationships. Some may need your influence and others you may need to walk away from.

Stolen Study Companion

JOURNAL NOTES:

Caroline Klug

SESSION 2:
The Slow Fade

You know the saying. You can't turn a ship on a dime. So it goes with our daily lives, and the choices that make up the paths we find ourselves on.

It's easy to look at someone else's choices and think we would never make the same ones. When we have this mindset, over one of grace, it opens a door for the enemy to challenge and tempt us. How does he infiltrate best? With compromise. He invites and tempts with situations that are less than desirable. Only, it typically begins as something so subtle, you barely recognize it as a big deal.

Compromise, enabled by desensitization, is a slow-growing disease that might seem innocuous at first, but soon begins to spread into every area of our lives. We are willingly accepting something less than what is right or beneficial. Little by little, the sum of our compromises begins to outweigh the "I'll never's," until we wake up one day and wonder how in the world we got to where we are.

Behind every compromise is a trigger. Something that starts us down the path, and typically takes the form of things like anger, disappointment, insecurity, grief, or even desire. Those types of emotions can disrupt our sense of self, and cause us to justify things that make us feel better. It's a slow and dangerous fade that can lead us far from God's intended path.

ALLEGORY COMPONENTS

Star/Sarah Judging Others
"A girl who had never crossed over to second base becoming a prostitute? It just wasn't going to happen." Star, Chapter 1

"Sarah gave the girl an apologetic look and excused herself from the warming well. She trotted quickly to the door, giving one look back at the girl who was watching her run away. Sarah wasn't sure what she thought of all of that but couldn't imagine making that kind of choice." Sarah with Cami Roberts outside the school, Chapter 6

Times when we look at someone else's situation and say "I'll never do that."

Choosing Her "John's"
"She had gotten in a lot of cars over the last year. Most were regulars, but when someone new showed up, she looked them over carefully, trying to decide if the situation would be safe. Well, safe enough." Star, Chapter 1

The compromises we make when we are desperate and willing to sacrifice best for good enough.

The more we get desensitized to what's around us, the more we compromise. Smaller becomes bigger, and innocuous becomes destructive.

Attraction to Jack
"Under any other circumstance, she might think he was attractive. But as it was, he was only a monster." Star, Chapter 3

Something bad looking attractive. The Bible tells us Satan masquerades as light (2 Corinthians 11:14). He can cause us to see things that are bad for us as attractive and alluring.

Also, when we become desensitized to early warning signs and discern danger only after an obvious attack.

It was easy for her to discern physical danger after being attacked and thrown into the prison, but when she first saw him, she ignored all the red flags. She was too desensitized to her environment to discern the spiritual danger, and her circumstances weakened her to compromise and engage with someone she might not otherwise have.

The Progression of Drugs to Prostitution
"Soon, crystal meth turned to heroin, and dancing could no longer pay for her addictions. In desperation, she hit

the streets. She was already broken, so what did it matter?" Star, Chapter 1

The day-by-day compromises and allowances we make which continually adjust our trajectory for the worse. Star started out taking pain killers from Ronny to dull the pain of dancing. Pills turned to meth, which turned to heroin, which ultimately turned to prostitution. It's an all-too-real example of the slow fade.

Star's Hindsight:
"Grief ripped through her as she flashed back to when she had let life swallow her whole." Star, Chapter 1

When working on *Stolen*, my editor initially thought I used the wrong word when I wrote "*let* life swallow her whole" but it was very intentional. This is a tougher part of the message, but we need to take accountability for the things we allow in our lives, and the consequences they bring.

Truth Behind the Lies

Matthew 26:41
Watch and pray so that you will not fall into temptation. The spirit is willing, but the flesh is weak.

2 Corinthians 11:14
And no wonder, for Satan himself masquerades as an angel of light.

1 Peter 5:8-9
Be alert and of sober mind. Your enemy the devil prowls around like a roaring lion looking for someone to devour. Resist him, standing firm in the faith, because you know that the family of believers throughout the world is undergoing the same kind of sufferings.

Hebrews 4:12
For the word of God is alive and active. Sharper than any double-edged sword, it penetrates even to dividing soul and spirit, joints and marrow; it judges the thoughts and attitudes of the heart.

Luke 6:37
Do not judge, and you will not be judged. Do not condemn, and you will not be condemned. Forgive, and you will be forgiven.

REFLECTION QUESTIONS

- Can you think of a time when you judged someone for something, and then found yourself in the same situation at some point later in your life?

- What compromises are most tempting to you? Is there any possibility there's a slow fade going on in that area?

- What kind of triggers cause you to fall into patterns and behavior that end up taking you farther away from the intended path? How are you using Scripture and your faith to keep those things from causing compromise in your life?

- Looking back, what are some examples of when God spoke softly to you, the still, small voice, and perhaps you didn't recognize it until later?

Stolen Study Companion

JOURNAL NOTES:

Caroline Klug

SESSION 3:
Under Fire

Attacks come in various forms. They can be consequences of poor choices, or they can be something that blindsides you and leaves you reeling.

The things you might bring on yourself are a bit like a double-edged sword. Not only are you wounded by the compromises themselves which bring you to a point of attack, but you're now faced with the fallout of those compromises, giving you a double serving of difficult.

For those things that simply happen *to* you, like the death of a loved one, the loss of a job, or false accusations, those attacks are unexpected. They disorient you, and leave you wounded along the side of the road, wondering what vehicle just hit you. I'm guessing it didn't feel like a bicycle.

How we respond *to* those attacks may dictate how long we stay *in* them. We can close our eyes and give in to what's trying to take us down, or we can close our eyes and pray to the One who can be our Protector and guide us out.

I know there might be times you feel weak or too wounded to fight back, but you serve an amazing God who can not only fight this battle for you (2 Chronicles 20:17), but who's already overcome whatever situation you find pressing down on you (John 16:33). Cry out to God for help, follow His guidance, and have peace knowing He is in complete control of the situation.

I would be remiss if I didn't mention one of the harder but more rewarding aspects of our attacks. If we keep our eyes and ears open, and our hearts malleable, we can learn a great deal and grow exponentially through our challenges. Although it might be difficult in the moment, that growth can help us avoid future attacks that might otherwise threaten us.

ALLEGORY COMPONENTS

The Abduction
Star being abducted by Jack in Chapter 1 represents the all too real attacks we face from the enemy every day.

Jack's Van
The larger picture of how the enemy can move us away from where we were, when we're too weak to fight.

Closing Her Eyes
"Maybe it was better not to fight. She closed her eyes, feeling herself fade into the blackness." Star, Chapter 1

When fighting back gets too hard, we get tempted to close our eyes and just give in to it.

Immoveable Objects
"Star looked around, looking for anything that could help her. Her bed frame was bolted to the cement floor, as was the chain to the wall." Star, Chapter 3

The hopelessness we sometimes feel within our own situations, and feeling like the things around us are immoveable objects.

Fatigue
"The fast walk was leaving her short of breath and her legs were already getting tired." Sarah, Chapter 12

Our spiritual walks, when we are not spending enough time in God's Word and in His presence.

Sarah had spent the last 5 years mostly confined to Jack's house, with little opportunity to exercise. She was out of shape and, because of that, tired easily on her walk to town. We need to condition ourselves to endure, so we can stand against the attacks of the enemy.

The Broken Mug
"When she held that mug in her hands, it would remind her of hope. It was one of the only things she had that reminded her there was something caring inside of Jack. As she was bent down collecting the pieces, she couldn't help but feel like this was somehow confirmation of what

life had become. What was once a symbol of hope was now only something broken." Sarah, Chapter 8

The things we find hope in outside of God. When those things shatter, we are left with only shards. When we place our hope in the things of this world, we will always be disappointed. When we place our trust in God, we can rest in the peace of knowing He is in control.

Scissors
The weapons we have at our disposal, such as the sword of the Spirt. The Word. Living and breathing and sharper than any double-edged sword.

Also, the things Satan uses to hurt us, but God can bring back around to help us.

TRUTH BEHIND THE LIES

Ephesians 6:11
Put on the full armor of God, so that you can take your stand against the devil's schemes.

2 Timothy 1:7
For the Spirit God gave us does not make us timid, but gives us power, love and self-discipline.

Matthew 19:26
Jesus looked at them and said, "With man this is impossible, but with God all things are possible."

Romans 8:28
> And we know that in all things God works for the good of those who love Him, who have been called according to His purpose.

2 Chronicles 20:17
> You will not have to fight this battle. Take up your positions; stand firm and see the deliverance the Lord will give you, Judah and Jerusalem. Do not be afraid; do not be discouraged. Go out to face them tomorrow, and the Lord will be with you.

REFLECTION QUESTIONS

- What are common ways people can feel spiritually attacked?

- Are you experiencing any of these kinds of attacks? If so, what things are you doing to fight the good fight?

- What types of "immoveable objects" do you see within your situation?

- How would you assess your level of spiritual fitness? If a new attack arose, would you be prepared to stand against the enemy or would you want to close your eyes and give in to it?

Caroline Klug

JOURNAL NOTES:

SESSION 4:
Controlling Forces

Merriam-Webster defines control as "to exercise restraining or directing influence over; To have power over." Whenever something restrains our abilities to do what we know is right, be that physically, mentally or emotionally, we can call that a controlling force – something that takes power away from us and causes us to make decisions we might know is not in our best interest. Those controlling forces can be a person, a drug, or even a bag of chips.

Besides Jack himself, one of the most significant examples of control in the novel is the heroin Star becomes addicted to. She called it her "constant intruder." In the last session we talked about the challenging attacks we face. It's hard enough to fight those battles as is. When we allow things into our lives that inhibit us, we greatly decrease our odds of survival or ability to fight the good fight.

Using things like drugs or alcohol not only puts us in harm's way, but it numbs us to the emotions of others. We see an example of this in Chapter 1 when Star ignores Lacey crying while she was engaged in her high. Once she came out of it, what did she feel? Guilt. It always seems good in the moment, but leaves us feeling dark emotions after the fact.

Did you know detachment can take on a form of control in our lives? Altering substances like heroin not only make you feel great, but cause you to feel detachment from the world around you.

There is something a bit more insidious which can creep in and cause an unhealthy detachment. Fantasies.

The mind is very powerful. When you choose to live in an alternate reality, one created in your head, that can produce negative consequences. Whether that comes in the form of avoidance or unhealthy fantasies involving other people, these habits can be something a person becomes addicted to. It's an escape not entirely different from a few glasses of wine or a mind-altering drug.

Jack's manipulation and Sarah's fear of facing what she was ashamed of were also two strong controlling forces, but we'll talk about those in the next few sessions, Lies We Believe.

Allegory Components

Shackles
The things we have in our lives that keep us tied up and unable to experience freedom.

Heroin and Pills
Anything used as a vehicle of detachment and/or leaves you debilitated, unable to be in control of your thoughts and actions.

Effects of the Heroin
Indulging in things that make us feel good in the moment, but take us farther from God.

While experiencing the drugs in her system it says Star felt "warm and safe." Not only is this a temporary feeling with negative long-term effects, but it's also a lie. Star was never warm and safe while she was high.

Star on the Floor
"She got up off the floor, staggered into the bedroom, and sat silently next to Lacey, combing her fingers through Lacey's tear-dampened hair." Star, after injecting herself with heroin, Chapter 1

Star didn't even take the time to sit on a chair, couch or bed before injecting herself, and spent her high time laying on what was probably a very dirty floor. This can represent the desperation we feel when we're not in control of ourselves.

Past Struggles
"I can see you're really struggling with the effects of the drugs leaving your system. I'm going to help you with that.... I give you small, periodic doses. It takes a little longer but will lessen the effects of your withdrawals." Jack to Star, Chapter 3

When Satan uses the struggles of our past to tempt us and bring us back to the same point of compromise.

Jack does this under the guise of helping her, as a means to wean her off her addiction. Isn't it just like Satan to use one of our past struggles to put us in a worse situation? If we don't get free, Satan will continue to use those things to control us.

Star/Sarah's Mental Retreats

"Star allowed the images in. The ones she kept hidden away for times when the heroin wasn't an option." Star, Chapter 3

"Sarah found herself smiling as she thought of Teddy." Sarah, Chapter 4

The fantasies we indulge in to escape reality or enable an alternate reality based on our desires.

Pain and Bleeding Caused by Shackles

How our shackles can make us feel both physically and spiritually. They continue to dig in and cause us pain until they are removed.

Reminder of Past Pain

"Jack got into the van but didn't start it right away. He just sat there. Sarah sat quietly, rubbing her fingers." After the Grocery Store Scene, Chapter 2

"Galia winced again at the reminder. She put her hand back in her lap, tucking her crooked fingers in between her thighs, out of view." Galia in the Prison with Rachel, Retelling When Her Fingers Were Broken, Chapter 18

Hiding the things that have caused us pain, keeping us both from the healing we need to move past it, as well as the opportunity of using it to help others.

Sarah was insecure with her crooked fingers. It wasn't just their appearance. There was a deeper sadness she relived when looking at them. It was one of her first go-to subconscious thoughts when she became afraid of Jack, exhibited by her rubbing her fingers. What thoughts do we tuck away because they are too painful to remember?

TRUTH BEHIND THE LIES

James 1:13-15
When tempted, no one should say, "God is tempting me." For God cannot be tempted by evil, nor does He tempt anyone; but each person is tempted when they are dragged away by their own evil desire and enticed. Then, after desire has conceived, it gives birth to sin; and sin, when it is full-grown, gives birth to death.

1 Corinthians 10:13
No temptation has overtaken you except what is common to mankind. And God is faithful; He will not let you be

tempted beyond what you can bear. But when you are tempted, He will also provide a way out so that you can endure it.

Philippians 4:8

Finally, brothers and sisters, whatever is true, whatever is noble, whatever is right, whatever is pure, whatever is lovely, whatever is admirable – if anything is excellent or praiseworthy – think about such things.

2 Corinthians 5:17

Therefore, if anyone is in Christ, the new creation has come: The old has gone, the new is here!

REFLECTION QUESTIONS

- What types of things do people indulge in that may make them feel good in the moment, but end up hurting them? Do you think something as simple as overeating can be a form of self-destruction?

- What things in your own life make you feel better, but might really be a form of self-destruction or self-sabotage? If you don't feel comfortable sharing, you can journal about it in the space provided.

- What do you use to mentally retreat from the world around you when things feel overwhelming or unbearable? Is it physical activity, alcohol, or like

Sarah, your imagination or fantasies? Do you think that form of detachment makes you the best version of you?

- If doing this in a group setting, share ideas on strategies for turning negative or unhealthy thoughts into positive, God honoring thoughts.

If you, or someone you know is struggling with a substance addition or another addiction that is physically threatening, please see the National Helpline topic within the reference materials section, for help, and seek help immediately.

Caroline Klug

JOURNAL NOTES:

SESSION 5:
Lies We Believe: Fear & Manipulation

This is the first of two sessions on lies we believe. Loved one, there's so much to talk about on this one, that we'll need more than one session to cover everything.

Manipulation is when someone alters our thoughts or actions for their own advantage, which is usually to our own detriment. Manipulation can be insidious. Gradually, over time, each carefully crafted lie or twisted intent comes together to form a transportation device that takes us far from the reality of the situation.

Fear is to manipulation what gasoline is to a vehicle. It's a match to a bonfire. When someone tells us something that causes us fear, our typical response is to want to run and hide, and avoid that threat at all costs. People can use that fear to steer us in a direction we may not have otherwise gone. Manipulation is like the shelter someone offers us when we're trying to hide from what we're afraid of.

The lies that were told in *Stolen* were evident. Some were blatant, like Jack saying he talked to Star's dad and there was a warrant for her arrest. Others were more insidious, like twisting his intentions and making her believe he was trying to help her. Can you see how the two worked together? The fear of being thrown in jail caused her to more readily accept when Jack offered her a home... a place to hide. Help that hurts and keeps things in the dark is no help at all, and we need to be quick to recognize when the enemy is at work.

Jack moved Star from one prison to another. The first was physical. The second was mental, and so much worse because she accepted it of her own free will. When Star left her physical prison, the shackle may have been removed, but a new and heavier one appeared in its place. When we run from the truth, secrets we choose to keep in the dark become an albatross that leads to death.

We can never allow Satan to manipulate us by convincing us we're better off in our prisons. It's not always easy to walk out of them, and sometimes we have to own up to the consequences of our decisions in order to do it, but in the end, there is freedom.

Allegory Components

Jack Wanting to Help Star
"Yes. I'm here to help you. It may not seem like it, but I'm here to save you." Jack, Chapter 3

Satan masquerading as light (something bad that he wants you to think is good). It also represents Satan's desire to mimic what God has and wants her to view him as her savior.

Jack Giving Sarah her Name
"He gave her another hard look up and down. 'How about Sarah? Yeah, I like Sarah. And you look like a Sarah. Let's go with that.'" Jack, Chapter 15

Allowing someone else to label you and tell you who you are or what you are. Or sometimes worse, what you're not.

When Satan mimics what God has, as the Bible tells us that God gives us a new name when we enter into the Kingdom of Heaven (Revelation 2:17).

Use of Father vs. Dad
When Satan tries to distance us from our heavenly Father or make us think our relationships with Him can't be intimate.

When talking about Eli Gregor, Galia always refers to him as "dad" whereas Jack uses the more formal title of "father." Jack's formality implies coldness and distance.

Scar on Sarah's Face
"'That will definitely leave a scar,' she said out loud. She ran her finger gently over the bandaged area, trying to imagine what it would look like. Sarah stared at her

reflection. She used to think she was pretty." Sarah, Chapter 2

The reflection of our inward beauty. Satan wants us to believe our beauty ends where our sins begin, giving us a false sense of self. A scar is permanent, representing no hope for change or redemption.

Jack Giving Sarah a Home
When Satan tries to take something dark and warped, and try to convince us it's the real deal. He takes a prison and makes us think it's protection.

Galia Not Trusting What She Knows of Her Dad
"I was scared, but I should have known better. I should have trusted what I know about my dad. About the kind of person I know he is." Galia to Rachel, regretting believing Jack's lies, Chapter 19

When we fail to trust the character of God and make decisions that are not in line with who the Bible says He is.

Truth Behind the Lies

Matthew 7:15
Watch out for false prophets. They come to you in sheep's clothing, but inwardly they are ferocious wolves.

1 Thessalonians 4:6
...and that in this matter no one should wrong or take advantage of a brother or sister. The Lord will punish all those who commit such sins, as we told you and warned you before.

2 Timothy 1:7
For the Spirit God gave us does not make us timid, but gives us power, love and self-discipline.

1 John 4:8
Whoever does not love does not know God, because God is love.

Ephesians 3:12
In Him and through faith in Him we may approach God with freedom and confidence.

REFLECTION QUESTIONS

- Can you think of a time you believed something about yourself that wasn't true, simply because someone else labeled you or told you that you should believe it?

- What negative things are you believing about yourself today, and what Scriptures can you find that show you the truth?

- God desires to have an intimate relationship with each of us. What thoughts or fears might keep you from believing or embracing this intimacy with God?

- Is there anyone in your life who's giving you the kind of help that hurts? If so, what can you do to bring that situation into the light?

If you, or someone you know is struggling with a situation that is physically or emotionally threatening, please see the National Helpline topic within the reference materials section, for help, and seek help immediately.

Stolen Study Companion

JOURNAL NOTES:

Caroline Klug

SESSION 6:
Lies We Believe: Shame & Denial

Shame and denial are powerful emotions, built on lies that keep us from experiencing true freedom.

I am convinced one of the deadliest weapons Satan uses against us is getting us to believe the truth will hurt us more than the lie. We get scared of admitting something we feel ashamed of, and hold on to the lies we think are protecting us, but are actually eating away at us from the inside out. The Bible tells us suppressing emotions like this can rot our bones (Psalm 32:3). In addition to the emotional agony, it can make us physically unhealthy.

Shame comes in two forms – the result of things that happen *because* of us and things that happen *to* us. It's usually obvious when bad things happen as consequences of our bad decisions. However, Satan also uses the things we have no control over. Star made the decision to run away, but she certainly didn't decide to get raped. That horrific act happened *to* her. Satan then fed her the lie that going home and telling her dad would only make things worse. Star was ashamed, and believed the lie that her dad would be too. Accepting that one lie altered the course of her entire life.

Denial is a coping mechanism that has dangerous long-term effects. The longer you deny something, the more lies that tend to accumulate. Pretty soon, you're in so over your head that the shame is intensified, and fear of being truthful feels that much more difficult.

Denial also has another purpose when looking at it as a coping mechanism. It enables avoidance and keeps us from dealing with something we know is a problem. That only hurts us, as well as others in our lives.

It can be terrifying to tell the truth, especially when we are the ones in the wrong, and we're afraid of what others might think of us because of what we did. Loved One, do not be manipulated by the enemy. No lie can overcome the truth, but truth can overcome any lie.

ALLEGORY COMPONENTS

The Rape

The traumatic things of this world that happen *to* us rather than *because* of us, but still have a significant impact on our trajectory, depending on how we choose to see and deal with them.

Lies Jack Told About Sarah's Dad
"I can't believe you'd be so stupid to think, of all of those people, your father would want you back. He hates you. He told me so. He knows what you did, and he's embarrassed by you. No. He's worse than embarrassed. He's ashamed." Jack, Chapter 2

In every instance we see of Galia, whether we see her as Star, Sarah, or Galia, Jack uses lies to manipulate her into thinking her dad is ashamed of her because of the prostitution and drugs. Satan uses shame as a weapon to weaken us and manipulate us into thinking we don't have other options.

Lies Jack Told Sarah About Herself
"'Why are you proud of me? I'm dirty. Unclean.' Eli looked at her, confused. 'Who told you that?' Galia looked down again. 'Jack.'" Galia and Eli, Chapter 20

The lies we believe because other people told us they were true. In Genesis 3:11, when Adam and Eve first felt embarrassed because they were naked, God asked them who told them that. The root of the shame they were feeling came from Satan.

Going to the Grocery Store
The hope and freedom of being out in the open. When we hide, it takes a toll on us. Going to the store was the only source of hope Sarah felt during the week.

Teddy's Suicide Attempt
The hopelessness of believing death is the only way to stop the pain we are experiencing.

Reliving Shame
"'He said because of being a part of...' Galia paused, reliving again the shame of her past with someone else."
Galia, Talking to Teddy, Chapter 20

Not healing from our past sins. Rather than receive the gift of forgiveness, we relive our shame every time we have to talk about it with someone new.

Tension Between Jack and Sarah
The constant tension between Sarah and Jack represent that gut punch from the Holy Spirit, telling you things are not okay. Deep down, Sarah knew that, but denied it. She convinced herself otherwise to avoid what she believed was something worse or more difficult.

Sarah Ignoring Signs of Jack's Role in the Abductions
When we recognize something is off or even sinful but we make excuses, because changing or confronting it is too hard or too inconvenient.

Sarah knew the man abducting women was Jack long before she admitted it out loud. Perhaps she feared it would force her to lose something she wasn't ready to give up.

Fear of the Police
"She was afraid to call the police. There were so many reasons it was a bad idea, but maybe they could help." Lacey, Chapter 1

"Where would she go? She wouldn't even be able to go to the police without getting herself in trouble." Sarah, Chapter 8

When we believe the lie that telling the truth will be more harmful than helpful.

Both Lacey and Sarah/Galia thought telling the truth would hurt them. It was ultimately what saved them.

Sarah Living a Life in Hiding
The sacrifices someone else convinces us are for our own good but are really hurting us.

The everyday life Sarah has with Jack is the result of her belief that she's sacrificing her personal desires to have "life." In reality, it's the sacrifices she's making that are taking her life away.

TRUTH BEHIND THE LIES

John 10:10
The thief comes only to steal and kill and destroy; I have come that they may have life, and have it to the full.

John 8:32
Then you will know the truth, and the truth will set you free.

Psalm 103:12
...as far as the east is from the west, so far has He removed our transgressions from us.

Psalm 34:5
Those who look to Him are radiant; their faces are never covered with shame.

Psalm 32:1-5
Blessed is the one whose transgressions are forgiven, whose sins are covered. Blessed is the one whose sin the Lord does not count against them and in whose spirit is no deceit. When I kept silent, my bones wasted away through my groaning all day long. For day and night Your hand was heavy on me. my strength was sapped as in the heat of summer. Then I acknowledged my sin to You and did not cover up my iniquity. I said, "I will confess my transgressions to the Lord." And You forgave the guilt of my sin.

REFLECTION QUESTIONS

- Describe what you think are some of the emotional, mental and even physical consequences of hiding something shameful.

- Can you think of a time when the Holy Spirit was trying to show you something, but you ignored what you were sensing, because of fear or perhaps not wanting to give something up?

- Has shame or guilt ever caused you to tell a lie? How did you feel after you told it?

- Have you ever come clean after telling a lie? Besides the fear and discomfort of working through that, how did you feel once everything was out in the open?

If you, or someone you know is struggling with thoughts of suicide, or have been a victim of sexual assault, please see the National Helpline topic within the reference materials section, for help, and seek help immediately.

Caroline Klug

Journal Notes:

SESSION 7:
Redemption

One of the intentional elements of this allegory has to do with Eli Gregor, Galia's dad. It's probably no secret he represents our heavenly Father, but when we look at the geography of the storyline, we uncover something surprising. Galia and her dad are originally from West Allis. When she was being held by Jack, she was in Greenfield, mere miles from West Allis. That whole time she was so close to her dad, and she didn't realize it.

Sweet One, you are never far from the Father, no matter where you're at, what you've done, or however big a wall you've put up. He's always there, ready to receive you with open arms.

When you look up redemption, it's derived from the word redeemed, which means to make up for something that would be considered a deficit. When Jesus died on that cross, He made up for every sin that ever was or ever would be committed. He endured the pain and death of the cross so we wouldn't have to. In doing so, He offers us the gift of forgiveness.

When we hold on to the guilt and shame of our past, we are not walking in the freedom that is found in God's forgiveness. That means we're not wholly and completely accepting forgiveness in the first place. Christ didn't offer forgiveness with the condition that we have to walk around under the weight and condemnation of our past. He tells us our sins are as far from us as the east is from the west (Psalm 103:12). We need only to let go.

Once we do, something beautiful happens. Not only can we experience a freedom like no other, but we can help others to do the same. Galia was only able to save Rachel because of what she had gone through. Just as Galia, you have things in your past which make you uniquely qualified and supernaturally called to help pull another from an ugly pit.

Helping others involves being transparent with our stories. I know that's hard. It can feel embarrassing and even terrifying. But recognize those too are lies from the enemy. If you truly believe you are not that person anymore, or that the things that have happened *to* you don't define you, then you can hold your head up high and trust that God will use every ounce of your story for His ultimate glory.

Allegory Components

Galia's "Final" Name
Galia is Hebrew for "redeemed." This name was reserved for who she ultimately became.

Saving Rachel
"Officers moved in to secure her. 'That's Galia! She saved me! She saved me!'" Rachel, Chapter 19

Being brave enough to fight against our own prisons can directly lead to the saving of another.

Eli's Joy of Reunion and Forgiveness
God's joy and heaven's celebration when someone who is lost is found, or comes to Jesus. It is also representative of the forgiveness God so freely and mercifully gives.

Galia's Testimony
How our testimony can help others who are or were in similar situations.

The Scars on Galia's Ankle
Healing from past emotional or spiritual trauma which can be used to help others. Physical evidence that someone made it through.

Galia's Location While With Jack
"Where are we? I mean, what town are we in?"
"All in good time, Sarah. All in good time."
Sarah and Jack, Chapter 15

Jack's house was only a few miles from where her dad lived, representing how close we are to the Father, no matter what our circumstances.

Eli Crying on TV
"Tears streamed down Galia's cheeks in grand succession. She was torn between exhilaration and guilt. Her choices were what had brought them to this moment they were indirectly sharing." Galia, crying watching her dad cry on TV, Chapter 16

God being with you every step of the way, feeling what you're feeling, and calling you to Him even in your darkest moment. He feels your pain.

Eli's Unconditional Love
"'I don't even know what to say, Dad. I was so worried you wouldn't want me back.' Eli laughed. 'That's because you're not a parent yet.' He grinned at her. 'Someday, I hope that you find out just what I'm talking about. Someday, I hope you realize the power of a parent's love, and how nothing you do can change that love.'" Galia and Eli, Chapter 20

God's unconditional love for us.

How Sarah Felt Reading Her Bible
"It [the Bible] felt like a fictional story, but she couldn't quite shake how she felt when she read it. It was the only time she didn't feel alone." Sarah, Chapter 2

God speaks to us in a lot of different ways. One of the most meaningful is His Word. It is active and alive (Hebrews 4:12), and even before Sarah truly understood its significance, she could still feel a supernatural power at work through the peace she felt reading it.

Truth Behind the Lies

John 11:35
Jesus wept.

1 John 1:9
If we confess our sins, He is faithful and just and will forgive us our sins and purify us from all unrighteousness.

Luke 15:10
In the same way, I tell you, there is rejoicing in the presence of the angels of God over one sinner who repents.

Hebrews 12:1
Therefore, since we are surrounded by such a great cloud of witnesses, let us throw off everything that hinders and the sin that so easily entangles. And let us run with perseverance the race marked out for us...

Psalm 107:1-2
Give thanks to the Lord, for He is good; His love endures forever. Let the redeemed of the Lord tell their story – those He redeemed from the hand of the foe...

Joshua 1:9
Have I not commanded you? Be strong and courageous. Do not be afraid; do not be discouraged, for the Lord your God will be with you wherever you go.

Reflection Questions

- What does your relationship with God look like when you are going through something difficult? Do you feel close to Him or far away?

- Where have you seen victory from past emotional wounds? What are some things that helped you get from an open wound to a healed scar?

- Do you feel you have wholly and completely accepted forgiveness for past sins? If not, what lies might you be believing that are keeping you from walking in freedom?

- Can you think of anyone in your life who might benefit from hearing your story? Prayerfully ask God for confirmation, and an opportunity to share.

Stolen Study Companion

JOURNAL NOTES:

Caroline Klug

But God...

I hope this study opened your mind to the ways the enemy might be at work, and encouraged your heart in the truth and power of redemption through Christ.

There was one important piece of the allegory we didn't cover within the sessions, because I wanted to save it for the end to leave you with something to think about.

Often times, we go through things we think are going to break us emotionally and kill us spiritually. For Star, that was the abduction experience. If you recall, there was a point she sat in her prison wondering if it might be better if Jack killed her – that maybe it was what she deserved. What she felt was hopelessness, and she couldn't see a way out. We can find ourselves in situations that make us feel the same way.

But God...

Those are two of my favorite words. But God. Whenever God is involved all bets are off. Nothing is hopeless.

> "Jesus looked at them and said, 'With man this is impossible, but with God all things are possible.'"
> Matthew 19:26

In hindsight, one might argue getting abducted might have been the best thing that happened to Star, because it got her off the streets and away from a life that would have surly killed her – either by the hands of another or eventually by the drugs. Granted, she choose to remain in her prison longer than she needed to, which caused more pain, but ultimately it was her path to freedom.

Here is the allegory, Sweet One. Sometimes, the thing we think is going to kill us is the very thing that ultimately saves us. The hard things we go through are what God knows we need, to get to a better place, no matter how hard or awful it might look to us.

Don't let the enemy convince you otherwise. When you see the influences of Satan around you, you need to kick, scream, fight, bite, and claw your way out from under him, and whatever he's using to pull you away from God.

Although Satan comes to steal, kill, and destroy, Jesus tells us that He comes to bring us life. When we chose to make Jesus our Lord and Savior, we're entering into an eternal covenant with Him. We learn in John 16:33 that even though Satan brings troubles all around us, Jesus has already overcome them. God wrote every day of our lives in His Book before any of them even happened. He knows every second of every one of your days. Whether it's this side of Heaven or not, He knows the ultimate victory will be His – and yours.

As you shake off the labels from those things that have happened to you, and wholly and completely accept God's forgiveness for those things that have happened because of you, you will see your wounds turn to scars. Scars are merely the evidence of once existing wounds, each with their own, unique story to tell. Your scars are not for you. They are for someone else to touch, to see that you made it through – to encourage them and strengthen them to know that they too can persevere (2 Cor 1:4).

The next time you find yourself encouraging someone else through a situation that you yourself once passed through, remember to praise God for your scars. They are evidence of His Glory and your redemption.

Caroline Klug

REFERENCE MATERIAL

Caroline Klug

NOVEL SUMMARY
* SPOILER ALERT *

Star is a teen runaway and prostitute. She's approached by Jack Price, who violently abducts her off the street and holds her captive in a remote prison in the woods. The abduction is witnessed by her roommate, Lacey, responsible for introducing Star to a life on the streets.

Star struggles to acclimate to her prison. Jack assures he wants to help her. Unbelieving, Star attempts an escape. It fails, leading to significant injury and depression. Through isolation, and fighting drug withdrawals, she recalls significant moments from her past – the death of her mother, Maggie Gregor, interactions with her father, Eli Gregor, her roommate, Lacey, and the series of unfortunate events ultimately bringing her face to face with her prison.

Revolving chapters weave her story around Sarah, the woman living with Jack. She sees a news broadcast about the abduction of a prostitute, Rachel McGinnis, which brings back the shame of her past. Sarah was a prostitute who Jack helped five years earlier. Their relationship is tense. Jack is controlling, and Sarah lives in fear of what Jack says will happen to her if she leaves. Sarah struggles with her own isolation, and escapes to thoughts of Teddy, her high school sweetheart.

Reinvigorated by hope, Star cooperates to gain Jack's trust, as a new means to escape. Jack shares there's a warrant for her arrest, her father wants nothing to do with her, and there are people from her ring looking to hurt her. This heightens Star's fears and she has a change of heart regarding Jack's intentions.

Sarah continues to follow news on Rachel. FBI Special Agent Emmanuel Grant is brought in to lead, as they uncover multiple cold cases with the same signatures. Sarah learns this is no longer a missing persons case, but one of a serial killer. Suspicions rise as she uncovers several connections and begins to suspect Jack is at the center.

Reeling from pain and confusion, Star now believes Jack wants to help her, and agrees to live with him as her only means to escape. Star is a street name, and she wants to go back to her real name, but Jack says she needs a new one for anonymity.

Sarah confronts the fears of her past and summons courage to leave the house in pursuit of truth. At this point, the chapters have been rotating between Star and Sarah. The reader thinks the scenes with Star is Rachel McGinnis' abduction playing out.

A twist is revealed that Star is Sarah, and her real name is Galia Gregor, daughter of Eli and Maggie Gregor. What readers have been reading is the history of how Galia ended up on the streets as Star, how she got from the prison to the house as Sarah, and why she chose to stay with Jack. The loop is closed on the connection between the two story lines, which are now merged and focused back on Galia. There are hints throughout, making subtle connections, but only fully understood once the twist is revealed.

Galia learns she is one of the cold cases, and her father's been looking for her. To help Rachel, she calls 9-1-1, but offers little information out of fear. Galia decides she needs to run from Jack and the police. She returns home for her things while wrestling with the idea of being back on the street. Galia struggles again with fear and doubt until she sees a news broadcast of her father giving an emotional plea. This displaces all the lies about her dad and fuels her courage to run, only to be caught by Jack at the last minute.

Jack ties Galia up and begins to unravel, revealing personal items tying him to the cold cases. Galia fears she's next. After another failed escape and brutal beating, Galia is brought back to the prison she started in as Star. She's not alone this time. Rachel's there, and the two girls ultimately fight to the death for their survival. Jack's death. The weapon ties back to something Galia originally left behind.

Based on various leads, Agent Grant and team locate Jack's property in the woods and arrive just after Jack is killed. Both girls are rescued and hospitalized. There is an emotional reunion scene with Galia, her father and Teddy, who is now a pastor.

Fast forward five years. Galia and Teddy are married. There is another emotional scene where Galia shares her story with Teddy's congregation, and talks about the physical and emotional prisons she lived in. Rachel McGinnis and her parents are present, along with Eli, Lacey and several of the women from the streets. Through a final exchange, Galia uses her pain to help another woman escape hers, bringing together the unexpected story of redemption – both for her and others.

Character Summary

Primary Characters

Galia Gregor a.k.a. Star, a.k.a. Sarah | 24 years old
Daughter of Eli and Maggie Gregor

Jack Price | 35 years old
Mill Worker, Abductor, Murderer

Teddy Fenton | 24 years old
Football Player, Galia's Best Friend, Pastor

Lacey | 24 years old
Prostitute, Star's Roommate

Ronny | 28 years old
Prostitution Ring Leader

Rachel McGinnis | 17 years old
Prostitute, Abductee

Eli Gregor| 46 years old
IT Programmer, Maggie's Husband, Galia's Dad

Maggie Gregor | 36 years old
Eli's Wife, Galia's Mom, Cancer Victim

Amy | 19 years old
Prostitute, Girl Galia Helps

Special Agent Emmanuel Grant | 45 years old
FBI Special Agent Assigned to Serial Abductions & Murders

Caroline Klug

Secondary Characters:

Annie | 17 years old
Prostitute, Jack's Sister, Murder Victim

Delilah | 28 years old
Receptionist in the Mill Where Jack Worked

Johnny | 22 years old
Jack's Co-Worker

Phil | 52 years old
Plant Manager; Jack's Boss

Emily | 18 years old
Prostitute; Annie's Best Friend; Jack's First Victim

Luke Reynolds | 50 years old
Local Police Chief

Amanda Kline | 16 years old
Prostitute; Murder Victim

Rhonda Shay | 17 years old
Prostitute; Murder Victim

Alexa Albert | 18 years old
Prostitute; Murder Victim

Cami Roberts | 16 years old
Prostitute; Girl at the warming well; Murder Victim

NATIONAL HELPLINES

National Suicide Prevention Lifeline
National Helpline: 1 (800) 273-8255

The Lifeline provides 24/7, free and confidential support for people in distress, prevention and crisis resources for you or your loved ones, and best practices for professionals.

SAMHSA: Substance Abuse and Mental Health Services Administration
National Helpline: 1 (800) 662-HELP (4357)

SAMHSA's National Helpline is a free, confidential, 24/7, 365-day-a-year treatment referral and information service (in English and Spanish) for individuals and families facing mental and/or substance use disorders.

National Sexual Assault Hotline
National Helpline: 1 (800) 656-HOPE (4673)

The national hotline, operated by RAINN (Rape, Abuse & Incest National Network), serves people affected by sexual violence. It automatically routes the caller to their nearest sexual assault service provider.

Caroline Klug

The Waiting Room
By Caroline Klug

Available on Amazon and Barnes & Noble.

If you're in need of a miracle, interceding for a loved one, or believing in God to move a mountain, getting on your knees is the easy part. The hard part is waiting. Not seeing the answers we long for can leave us feeling depressed and even doubtful. We begin fixing our eyes on the world around us, rather than the One who made the world.

Whether it's been a day or a decade, don't lose hope. You serve a mighty God, capable of doing immeasurably more than you could ever ask or imagine (Ephesians 3:20). Join me as we dive into God's Word for insights and reassurance during your wait. He has a plan for your life, and His timing is always perfect.

Caroline Klug is an author of inspirational fiction, using thrillers and short story collections as a way to bring insights to people all over the world.

In addition to fiction, Caroline writes Christian Living books that teach, inspire, and encourage.

To see other books by this author visit:
www.CarolineKlug.com

Caroline Klug

www.ingramcontent.com/pod-product-compliance
Lightning Source LLC
Chambersburg PA
CBHW071220070526
44584CB00019B/3088